NEW YORK

CITY OF MANY DREAMS

Featuring the photography of

Robert Van Der Hilst

CLB 978
© 1987 Illustrations and text: Colour Library Books Ltd.,
    Guildford, Surrey, England.
Text filmsetting by Acesetters Ltd., Richmond, Surrey, England.
Printed and bound in Barcelona, Spain by Cronion, S.A.
All rights reserved.
1987 edition published by Crescent Books, distributed by Crown Publishers, Inc.
ISBN 0 517 40547 4
h g f e d c b a

NEW YORK

CITY OF MANY DREAMS

Text by Bill Harris

Produced by
TED SMART and DAVID GIBBON

CRESCENT BOOKS

Part of the decoration in the lobby of the Empire State Building in New York City consists of illustrations of the Seven Wonders of the World at the time of Alexander the Great. When the building was finished in 1931 it was widely hailed as the eighth wonder of the world, but students of antiquity knew that the natural successor to the original seven had already been a part of the New York scene since 1886. And of the many dreams that are the fabric of New York, nothing is symbolic of more of them than the statue that stands in the harbor, Frederic-Auguste Bartholdi's *Liberty Enlightening the World.*

One of the ancient Wonders, the Colossus of Rhodes, also overlooked one of the world's great harbors and was placed there as a symbol of the spirit and creativity of a nation. It was also remembered for centuries as the biggest and best of the great colossal statues. But it was a full 50 feet shorter than the lady in New York harbor. Even Nero's spectacular monument to himself in Rome was 30 feet shorter. The Statue of Liberty, from the tip of her toe to the top of her torch, is 151 feet, one inch high. Along with the pedestal, the whole monument rises to a height of 305 feet, six inches.

Since October 28, 1886 when President Grover Cleveland officially accepted this gift of the people of France, the statue has consistently been among New York's top five tourist attractions and, except for the Brooklyn Bridge, which pre-dates it by five years and three months, it is the oldest landmark synonymous with the city itself.

But the Statue of Liberty is more than a symbol of New York City. It is a landmark of the American dream. And it stands less than a half mile away from the second greatest landmark of the same dream, Ellis Island.

The immigrant station at Ellis Island was formally opened on January 1, 1892 when a transfer boat carrying 148 steerage passengers from the S.S. *Nevada* pulled in to its new pier. Annie Moore, a 15 year-old girl from Ireland was first to set foot on the island as an immigrant. Before it was closed as a reception center in 1932, more than 16 million souls had followed in her footsteps.

In its final year the Ellis Island facility processed 21,500 immigrants. In its peak year, 1907, 1,285,349 were admitted.

During World War II and up until its final closing in 1954, Ellis became a detention and deportation center and some German aliens were held prisoner there, in the shadow of the Statue of Liberty, for all of the war years. It was possibly because of that final bitter memory that the Eisenhower Administration declared the island surplus in 1956 and offered it for sale to the highest bidder. The announcement at least had the sensitivity to refer to it as "one of the most famous landmarks in the world."

None of the bids and proposals proved high enough. The highest was an offer of close to $2 million offered by a New York developer who wanted to build a mini-city on the 27½-acre island and had even provided designs by the great American architect Frank Lloyd Wright.

Such proposals were laid to rest in 1965 when President Lyndon B. Johnson proclaimed Ellis Island and the Statue of Liberty partners in a National Monument. His proclamation included plans for restoration which have yet to be realized.

Almost two decades later, a new Administration in Washington with strong faith in "the private sector" decided ordinary citizens should contribute the money necessary to do the job as well as fund desperately needed repair work on the Statue of Liberty herself.

It's not an unprecedented request. The Statue was built with funds donated by French citizens, but the million francs they raised wasn't enough to build a base for it in New York. A subscription drive on this side of the Atlantic produced enough to build 15 feet of masonry, but the Statue was doomed to stay in 214 crates in a Paris warehouse for more than a year while Joseph Pulitzer used the editorial page of his *New York World* to convince New York citizens that their pennies and dimes mattered in making this part of the dream come true.

The Island of Manhattan across the Bay has been a symbol of dreams since Henry Hudson first took word of it back to the Dutch East India Company in 1609. "It is as beautiful a land as one can hope to tread upon," he told them. With typical Dutch caution, it took them four more years to send Adriaen Block to see if Hudson was telling the truth. It took them another eight years to change their name to the Dutch West India Company and declare the territory their private preserve.

Their original settlement was on present-day Governor's Island. But the way Washington Irving's Diedrich Knickerbocker tells the tale, they missed the point and put their first settlement in the New Jersey swamps. If you take his word for it, that's where the great city would be today if a party of explorers led by Oloffe Van Kortlandt had not been shipwrecked on the western shore of the East River about where the end of 89th Street is today, the spot where the Mayor's official residence, Gracie Mansion, is located. And, according to Father Knickerbocker, they'd have gone home completely unimpressed had not Van Kortlandt dreamed a dream.

"... And, lo, the good St. Nicholas came riding over the tops of the trees in that selfsame wagon wherein he brings his yearly presents to children," wrote Irving in his description of Oloffe's vision. "... The shrewd Van Kortlandt knew him by his broad hat, his long pipe and the resemblance he bore to the figure on the bow of the Goede Vrouw (the ship which had brought them to the New World). And he lit his pipe by the fire and he sat himself down and smoked; and as he smoked the smoke from his pipe ascended into the air and spread like a cloud overhead. And the sage Oloffe hastened and climbed up to the top of one of the tallest trees, and saw that the great volume of smoke spread over a great extent of country – and as he considered it more attentively, he fancied that the great volume of smoke assumed a variety of marvelous forms, where in dim obscurity he saw shadowed-out palaces and

domes and lofty spires, all of which lasted a moment, and the whole rolled off and nothing but the green woods were left. And when St. Nicholas had smoked his pipe he twisted it in his hatband, and laying a finger beside his nose he gave the astonished Van Kortlandt a very significant look; then mounting his wagon he returned over the treetops and disappeared."

When the explorers got back to their settlement across the Hudson, their fellow citizens agreed that St. Nicholas indeed intended them to settle the Island of Manhattan and that Van Kortlandt was "... a most useful citizen and a right good man – when he was asleep."

The truth is that the merchants in New Amsterdam didn't need a dream to convince them that there were riches beyond their own wildest dreams waiting for them on this tiny island. In 1626 they dispatched Peter Minuit with instructions to buy the place. The deal was made in front of a fort the Dutch were building at the present-day site of the Custom House on Bowling Green. The price was 60 Guilders, well known in today's money as twenty-four dollars. The deal has often been referred to as one of the slickest real estate transactions in history. But two years later, Minuit paid roughly the same price to the same Indian tribe for all of Staten Island. Manhattan is 14,211 acres, compared to Staten Island's area of 36,600 acres. Three years after that the Dutch fired Peter Minuit for being overly-generous and he went into the service of the Swedish Government, in whose behalf he bought most of Delaware, including the present site of Wilmington, for one copper pot.

But if New York has always been a mecca for opportunists, it has been important from the very beginning to the dreams of people looking for opportunity. The Dutch settled their colony here with refugees from Belgium who had migrated to Holland looking for religious freedom and, having found it, then wanted more in the way of financial betterment. Dutch was the official language of New Amsterdam, but before its population reached 500 it was reported that eighteen different languages were spoken there.

That was just the beginning.

By the end of the 17th century, the English had taken over but the Dutch didn't move away. The result was that New York became America's first truly international city and the stage was set to make it a key element in what would soon become known as "the American dream."

When the Dutch moved to America their basic goal was what historians call economic opportunity. They came to make money. When the English took over their idea was essentially the same. Until the Revolutionary War, Boston had been, along with Philadelphia, the major port of entry for merchandise exported by the great British merchants. Unfortunately for them, both Boston and Philadelphia suffered a bad press in England during the war years. But New York was in British hands during most of those years and when it was all over it became the favored port of the English merchant fleets. By 1815, the value of imports coming into New York Harbor was more than double that of Boston and three times that of Philadelphia.

At the same time New York became established as the best place for immigrants to head for, simply because there were more jobs there. Then, ten years later, in 1825, the Erie Canal connected New York with the riches of the West. From that moment on, New York could truly be called a city of many dreams.

An immigrant who put his dream to work in a spectacular way was a young man who arrived here from Waldorf, Germany, in 1784. His name was John Jacob Astor. He married a local girl a year later and used his bride's dowry to get into the fur business. By the beginning of the new century he had already amassed a fortune of a quarter of a million dollars, some of which he used to get into the China trade. He sent his ships from New York around the tip of South America to Oregon, where he had established a colony he modestly called Astoria. They went to China from there loaded with furs from the Pacific Northwest and completed the circle by coming back to New York loaded down with tea and silk. In the process Astor became the richest man in New York City. By 1840 he was known around town as "New York's landlord," with 355 pieces of property, all fully rented.

In 1850, two years after Astor died, P.T. Barnum paid the unheard-of rent of $500 a week for Castle Garden, the converted fortress at the edge of Battery Park, to introduce his latest "discovery," the Swedish soprano Jenny Lind.

By today's standards it was a low price. The theater could seat 6000, only a handful less than the capacity of Radio City Music Hall, the biggest theater in the world today. But it was a fortune to Barnum, who announced he would hold an auction for tickets to the Swedish Nightingale's opening night. The auction, held in Castle Garden, was attended by 5000 people, each of whom had paid a "bit" (half a quarter) for the privilege of being there. Only one thousand tickets were auctioned but Barnum collected $10,141 for his afternoon's work. Many of the people who put in successful bids turned a nice profit, too. The event gave birth to an institution that has existed ever since. The tickets were resold by these first scalpers in the park outside on opening day.

All the greats of the world of entertainment appeared at Castle Garden during its years as a theater, from song writer Stephen Foster to dancer Lola Montez. It was the scene of band concerts and operas, political rallies and Shakespearean productions, variety shows and important debates.

Then, on August 3, 1855, Castle Garden became America's first reception center for immigrants. In the next thirty-five years and eight months, 7,690,606 would pass through the doors of the former theater, an average of eighteen hundred a month. In the days before the Civil War, nearly all of the immigrants arrived in sailing ships and the vast majority of them had little stomach for traveling any further once they got to New York, in spite of the common advice in Europe that they should avoid the cities once they arrived in America.

In the thirty years before New York opened that formal immigration reception center, the city's population had grown from 166,000 to 630,000. And it had long since taken on the cosmopolitan attitude it has never lost. In the 1830s a visiting European was astounded to find strolling along Broadway: ". . . people of color, Germans and Dutch, Irish, French, Danes, Swiss, Welsh, English, Scots, Italians, Turks, Chinese, Swedes, Russians, Norwegians, Poles, Hungarians, Spaniards, Sicilians, Africans and, in short, a few of all the nations upon the earth."

Castle Garden has taken back its original name, Castle Clinton, and is now, like Ellis Island and the Statue of Liberty, a National Monument. But there are other, less formal, memorials to the immigrants, many of which still serve the immigrants of today: the tenements of the Lower East Side.

New arrivals to New York in the 19th century generally spent their first nights in boarding houses near the docks. Often whole families were packed into a single room. Ideally, the arrangement was only temporary and as soon as they were able they moved on to more permanent quarters. But in some cases they went from bad to worse.

The huge waves of Irish immigrants who arrived in the 1840s moved into an area at the western edge of today's Chinatown. Their community of run-down buildings, including an abandoned brewery, and tar paper shacks, was known as Five Points. Charles Dickens said of it, "... debauchery has made the very houses prematurely old." It was an area controlled by violent street gangs whose victims were lucky if they could get away with nothing more than having an ear or a nose bitten off or an eye deftly gouged out. In later years, Al Capone bragged that nothing in Chicago was a match for him because he had grown up in Five Points.

As soon as they could, the Irish moved slightly east and north into the areas that are called Chinatown and Little Italy these days. They left their former homes to the Germans and Poles, English and Italians who followed them to the New World.

Among the newer arrivals, the Germans were the first to pick up stakes and move on. They moved into the area north of City Hall and south of 14th Street, known today as the Lower East Side. In the 1850s their presence gave it the name "Klein-Deutschland," Little Germany. They held sway there until after the turn of the century, giving up only the portion of their territory below Houston Street to the waves of Jewish immigrants who were beginning to arrive from Russia and Romania. The quarter became almost all Jewish after the Germans began moving uptown above 83rd Street (displacing the Irish, by the way) after the first subway was built in 1904.

Ironically, the uptown neighborhood, called Yorkville, is commonly thought-of as a German community; the Lower East Side is considered Jewish. But neither of them could claim the label until only 75 years ago.

The second generations of immigrant families didn't feel the need to cling to their own ethnic groups and dispersed elsewhere, leaving the old ghetto-like neighborhoods to other new arrivals. The first waves moved away from Manhattan and into the other Boroughs of New York City and though many of them are raising their children there today, they are increasingly surrounded by people who, like their grandparents, find the English language bewildering and the American way of life the object of a dream that's difficult to grasp.

And, like the earlier immigrants, this new wave, the biggest since the 1920s, seeks the companionship of people who speak their language and share their customs. Immigrants from Mainland China have expanded the borders of Chinatown to the consternation of the people across Canal Street in Little Italy where signs in shop windows are more and more likely to be Chinese ideograms, and the restaurants are as likely to feature lemon chicken as chicken cacciatore. New arrivals from the Middle East or from the Caribbean are likely to find a touch of home in Brooklyn. But among the new ethnic outposts, the one that outdoes them all is a little community in Queens not far from LaGuardia Airport that provided escape from the city for the English and Dutch in Colonial times, the neighborhood called Elmhurst.

At the beginning of 1982, the U.S. Immigration and Naturalization Service reported that there were 650,000 legal immigrants living in the five Boroughs of New York City. On top of that, city agencies estimate that there are 750,000 aliens living in New York who got here by other than legal means and therefore are not counted in official tallies. All of them have one thing in common: the famous American dream. They're here to make it big and some of them will. Meanwhile, just "making it" is the order of the day.

Out in Elmhurst, a cop on the beat says "... anything God put on this earth, we've got two of them right here in the 110th Precinct." And at Public School 89, whose 1600 young students were born in 50 different countries, only about a third of the kids will tell they are "American" rather than Korean, Columbian or Yugoslavian; but almost none will say they'd like to go back to where they were born. "It's better over here," says one, "we've got sports, video games, movies." Their parents know they've got much more and that, by and large, is why they're here with a dream and a desire. And why they probably will never go back.

But New York attracts more than just immigrants and ordinary job-hunters. Even though the unemployment rate among young people is higher in New York than in some other parts of the country and increasing numbers of people have been leaving the cities of the Northeast for the climate and opportunities in the Southwest, there's a segment of the population of America that knows the only way to make their fondest dreams come true is to come to New York.

Their average age is 22 to 29 years old. They're college-educated. They're eager, even excited. And over the past 15 years they've migrated to New York in increasing numbers, making themselves one of the fastest-growing segments of the City's population and giving New York America's biggest net-increase in citizens of that age group.

Traditionally, young people migrating to New York have been aspiring actors and artists, musicians and writers. And they're still arriving every day of the week. But in the last few years, more and more young people have been coming to New York in search of a business career. Some of them are young lawyers, others have fresh MBA diplomas tucked into their briefcases. Often as not they'll say that they chose New York not just because there are better jobs for them here, but because the on-the-job training they'll get will make them more valuable back where they came from.

But when they get here, something strange happens. They themselves provide a spark to the New York atmosphere that no other city has. Then the spark turns to fire and before you know it, they're hooked. Peoria never ever looks that attractive again.

Obviously, one of the things that makes New York so attractive to them is the other people in the same age group they meet and share their dreams with. An artist who came to experiment, an actor who works part-time as a waiter to give him more time to go to auditions and classes, a music student who makes ends meet by giving impromptu recitals on a Fifth Avenue street corner, all have one very important thing in common: each other. They find the diversity exhilarating, too. They give New York a huge measure of its vitality and excitement and that's precisely what they came here to find, not to mention what keeps them here.

But if there is so much dreaming going on in New York, why is everyone so wide awake? Probably the best reason is because so many of those dreams are coming true. It's possible to be successful in places like Los Angeles or Chicago, of course, but there's a certain pride that goes along with being a success in New York that makes it something special. Though people on the way up will usually tell you that this kind of pride is the prize they're after, you know that's about the same as a student who says he's after a medical degree because he wants to help people.

The thing that makes the world go around in New York is money, and there are more ways to make more of it than just about any other spot on earth. In earlier generations, the road to success was usually paved on the playing fields of the right schools and in quiet recesses of the right clubs. But these days, more often than not, the key to success is being in the right place at the right time. The right place right now happens to be New York.

It's a place where two people can bump into each other on the street and in less than five minutes change the direction of their lives. It's a place where a young person can get noticed, where new ideas can get accepted. If Horatio Alger were alive today, his stories would have to be about New Yorkers.

The reason why it all works is because there are so many people working at it. There are more than 23,000 people per square mile in New York, and that's just those who live here. The Monday-Friday working environment is so densely packed with people who commute from every direction to jobs in New York that on weekends, when the suburbanites all stay home, the people who live in New York feel almost lonely.

On weekends they worry less about "gridlock" – that threatened menace traffic experts predict will happen on the day when crosstown traffic blocks all the up and downtown intersections and everybody just gets out of their car and walks away. They don't worry at all about finding parking places, which is much easier on Saturdays and Sundays, because Manhattanites, at least, quite unlike any other segment of the American population, don't own cars. Insurance rates are higher, monthly parking costs more than two-bedroom apartments in other cities and the average speed of traffic on weekdays is under ten miles an hour. Besides, when you live in New York, where else is there to go?

That's not to say Manhattanites are homebodies. There are probably more telephone answering machines in New York City than any place else, and more calls received by them from coin-operated telephones which can be found on nearly every street corner in town.

If they're not home much, it's surely not because their homes come cheap. At any given time, less than two per cent of the apartments in Manhattan are vacant and on any given weekend it's not uncommon for people who have been apartment-hunting for a year or more to walk the streets of desirable neighborhoods knocking on random doors in hopes that someone living there might be thinking about moving soon. The answer is usually "no," but that doesn't discourage them.

Because there is a shortage, rents are high. Depending on the desirability of the neighborhood, a $600-a-month apartment is a rare bargain and two small rooms could easily cost twice that much. Rents are usually quoted on a per-room basis, but because of a law that limits the size of increases in rent when new leases are signed, one-room apartments, called "studios," sometimes cost more than two-bedroom units in the same building. The reason is that smaller apartments get new tenants more often and more new leases mean more periodic increases in the rent.

One of the reasons for the shortage is that a huge number of New York apartment buildings have "gone co-op" – which means that the owners have sold them apartment-by-apartment to their tenants or to outsiders. In that way, New Yorkers have gotten to share one of the basic American dreams: owning their own home. But they pay a high price for the privilege. The value of a typical one-bedroom apartment in a Manhattan high-rise building is about $200,000. In lesser cities that kind of money would buy a mansion. And in lesser cities a mansion bought with that kind of money would be all yours to do with as you please. But a Manhattan cooperative apartment isn't the same thing as a mansion in Mason City, Iowa. Buying it usually involves the same down payment and the same agonizing negotiations with a bank to convince them that you are a solid citizen worthy of borrowing money at 20 per cent interest. But the similarity ends there. In New York you have to be scrutinized by the co-op board, a body made up of other people who own apartments in the building you've chosen. They usually take the selection of new neighbors very seriously. In recent celebrated cases, former President Richard Nixon didn't pass muster with the board of a Fifth Avenue building and Gloria Vanderbilt, a person who could surely afford the mortgage payments, was denied the right to live under the same roof with the people who live in an elegant East Side building.

Co-op owners need to budget themselves for more than mortgage payments. There's an added monthly cost called "maintenance." The amount is set by the board and is based on the costs of running the building. There are heating and lighting bills to think about, a staff to be paid. In buildings with 24-hour doormen and elevator operators, the payroll can be steep. In older buildings or newer ones that are poorly built, lots of money needs to be collected from all the owner-tenants to keep the place ship-shape. There are taxes to be paid, and insurance. If someone in the building decides it would be nice to have heating elements installed in the building marquee to make winter comings and goings more pleasant, everyone in the building pays for it as long as the board agrees it's a good idea.

The result is that maintenance charges are subject to change and it's possible that people living in a co-op building could get a letter tomorrow morning that their monthly bill is going to be increased by $200 a month, effective right away, because the board had a meeting last night and decided that is the way it has to be.

Naturally, a co-op owner has the right to move out in the face of such a development. It's a free country, after all. But to move you first have to sell the apartment and to sell it you have to find a buyer the board will approve. While you're looking it's probably a good idea to stay away from the likes of Gloria Vanderbilt or Richard Nixon.

When the former president was told he wasn't welcome as the owner of a co-op apartment, he took the alternative of buying an entire house. The neighborhood he chose was on the East Side of Manhattan where at the time the lowest price for what they would call a "handyman's special" in suburban communities was $1 million. The "value" has gone up considerably since then and the cost of a four-storey townhouse in any desirable Manhattan neighborhood is well over $2 million and there are buyers waiting in line.

What you get for your investment in a New York rowhouse is often the chance to become a landlord and produce some income to help offset the monthly payments.

In the 19th century everyone in New York lived in four-storey houses except the very poor and newly-arrived immigrants who lived in tenement buildings. Because those multi-unit buildings were associated with the lower classes, it wasn't until after the Civil War that middle- and upper-class people took to the idea of "flats," and the early examples were designed to include all the amenities people expected in private homes.

Though they look different, the charming little houses in Greenwich Village were built on the same basic plan as the later palaces on the Upper East Side. The first floor was built up off the ground following a custom established by the first settlers from Holland who couldn't help worrying about floods. The floor was reached by a set of outside steps called a "stoop" after the Dutch word for step. Under the steps there was an entrance to a ground level floor that had a kitchen in front and a laundry room in the rear. The kitchen was placed there as a convenience to the grocer and butcher who could make deliveries without actually intruding on a family's living space. The laundry was done in back as a convenience to the maid who had to get the water to do the washing from a well in the back yard.

Most 19th-century New York families had at least one servant, usually a maid, because there were so many young immigrants who were as grateful for the job as for a place to live. The servants shared quarters with the young children of the family on the top floor under the roof. The floor just beneath it contained two bedrooms. The owner of the house and his wife took that for themselves because it was quieter and overlooked the garden in back. The front bedroom was reserved for the older generation, the parents of the owner or some other relative, who were probably deaf and didn't mind traffic noises in the street outside.

The floor reached from the stoop was the parlor floor and every early New York house had two parlors. The one in front was kept neat and tidy as a place to entertain friends and neighbors who usually dropped in without notice back in those days before there was a telephone. The back parlor with its view of the back yard was reserved for family evenings at home and, though less elegant, was usually much more cozy and comfortable.

Though all 18th- and 19th-century New York houses were simple wood frame buildings, often faced with brick, all of them are loosely called "brownstones" today. The term comes from a type of sandstone common in the New Jersey hills. After the first brownstone-faced house, the rectory of the Church of the Ascension, was built on West 10th Street in 1840, the material became all the rage. It was soft enough to be easily cut and stone yards in New Jersey were kept busy for the next 60 years pre-fabricating balustrades, ornate lintels to grace windows and doorways, and entire facades for elaborate Anglo-Italian town houses which became the last word in private housing in New York both literally and figuratively.

There are about 400 of these "true brownstones" left in Greenwich Village today, including the one at 6 Saint Luke's Place where Mayor Jimmy Walker lived from the time he was five years old. Though "Gentleman Jim's" father was a doctor, their neighbors, by and large, were middle class tradespeople back in 1886 when the Walkers moved in. Their lives generally fell into a comfortable routine, the highpoint of the week being a stroll or a drive through the new Central Park which had been formally opened in the 1860s. In the years before that the most popular Sunday afternoon excursions were to a park that wasn't even in New York City. It was a place called "The Elysian Fields" across the Hudson River in Hoboken, New Jersey.

The park had been created by Colonel John Stevens, founder of the Stevens Institute of Technology, which still overlooks the river near the former site of his park. Stevens owned just about all of Hoboken in those days and he was eager to see it developed. As an encouragement for potential builders and buyers, he instituted New York City's first Hudson River ferry in 1811. It ran from the end of Barclay Street to Hoboken. The problem was that nobody wanted to go to Hoboken. Stevens solved that by turning a portion of his own estate into a public park.

The Main Event for visitors was lining up for hours for a chance to ride on the Colonel's private railroad, a little train that took seven passengers at a time on a circular route through the park. It was the first and only railroad in the United States whose train was pulled by a steam engine rather than horses.

But the park itself was the real attraction. Mrs. Trollope, the great English chronicler, hopped the ferry in 1832 and came back very impressed. "It is hardly possible to imagine a place of greater attraction," she wrote. "A broad belt of light underwood and flowering shrubs, studded at intervals with lofty forest trees, runs two miles along a cliff which overhangs the matchless Hudson. Sometimes it feathers the rocks down to its very margin and at others leaves a pebble shore, just rude enough to break the gentle waves and makes a music which mimics softly the loud chorus of the ocean. Through this beautiful wood, a broad, well-gravelled terrace is led past every point which can exhibit the scenery to advantage. Narrower and wilder paths diverge at intervals, some into the deeper shadows of the woods, some shelving gradually to the pretty coves below. The price of entrance to this little Eden is the six cents you pay at the ferry."

New Yorkers today find it tough to believe that Mrs. Trollope's Eden could possibly be Hoboken, New Jersey, even though the city has become immensely popular with people looking for good housing at a fraction of Manhattan's real estate prices.

What God and man created together on the cliffs of Hoboken, man took it upon himself to do in 1858 when architect Calvert Vaux and his friend from Staten Island, Frederick Law Olmstead, submitted what they called "The Greensward Plan" and won a design competition for the creation of a huge park at the northern edge of the settlement in Manhattan.

The area that had been selected for this "Central Park" was a mess in the 1850s when the City bought the land. It was studded with boulders and meandering streams. It was littered with squatters' shacks and little farms. In the middle of it all, where the Great Lawn is today, north of 81st Street, was a huge reservoir that had outlived its usefulness but represented a big saving in land-acquisition costs.

Olmstead and Vaux proposed tearing it all apart and starting over. Near the present corner of 59th Street and Fifth Avenue they said they would convert a dry creek bed into a pretty pond. A little further north and west, where the rock outcrops were formidable, they decided they'd get rid of the rocks and replace them with a meadow which would even have grazing sheep. Up at 74th Street, they would, they said, turn a stream into a lake. It would be a perfect terminus for the broad Mall they had planned just east of the Sheep Meadow. To give strollers the impression that the 840-acre park was bigger, they planned a few little tricks to fool the eye. One of them was to build the miniature Belvedere Castle on an axis with the Mall at the top of a rock outcrop six blocks away. Because

of its small size and massive proportions it would look more like it was six miles away. Explaining the creation of the lake, Vaux wrote: "Fifty feet of water will give an idea of distance and of difficulty in passing it greater than 500 feet of ground will."

The whole project was the result of a dream by poet William Cullen Bryant, who was connected with the New York Post in those days and used its pages to share the dream with his neighbors. He was enthusiastically joined by authors George Bancroft and Washington Irving. Together they were able to convince the City Fathers it was a dream well-worth dreaming. Before they were through, Central Park would cost more than $300 million, translated into today's dollars. But there is not a man, woman or child in the City of New York today who would not agree it was worth every penny.

The builders had their work cut out for them. It would be an awesome engineering feat even today. In the middle of the 19th century dynamite hadn't been invented yet, not to mention jackhammers, bulldozers and dumptrucks. All they had was black powder explosives to blast the rocks, and human brawn and horses to haul the debris away. The lakes and new streams had to be dug with picks and shovels. Thousands of trees had to be planted by hand.

The size of the labor force varied during the ten years it took to do the job. In 1862, when 74,370 trees and shrubs were planted, 3800 men were kept busy as were 400 horses. In that year alone they exploded 250,000 pounds of black powder.

All together 3,583,128 cubic yards of stone and dirt were moved to create the seemingly natural setting that became Central Park. And except for some encroachments like the ever-expanding backside of the Metropolitan Museum of Art, the park looks very much the same today as it did when the first bicycle riders began appearing there in the 1890s. Early users of the park never dreamed about skateboards and blaring radios, but in the 1870s they did a lot of complaining about millionaires like Leonard Jerome and August Belmont who used the park's drives as racecourses to get their horses warmed up for the big races they staged on the wide avenues of Harlem.

Visitors to the city, and even some New Yorkers themselves, miss the experience of Central Park because they've been told it isn't safe to go there. Statistically, it's one of the safer areas in a city that is itself safer than a dozen other smaller cities in the United States. To be sure, there are people everywhere who will prey on other people they consider vulnerable. The myth about Central Park being a hotbed of muggers and other anti-social characters probably comes from the fact that it is such a natural sylvan setting. People instinctively feel safer in natural surrounding than on a city street and every time that instinct is challenged, it is noticed more. People who choose to believe that the park is best avoided on a warm spring day when the lawns are covered with daffodils, or a crisp fall day when the elms along the Mall turn a wonderful shade of yellow, are missing out on one of the best things about New York.

The urban historian Henry Hope Reed once wrote that "Central Park is the greatest single improvement made in any American city in the course of the nation's history. No other work of art . . . has had such influence; only the national Capitol building in Washington has had more. From Central Park have sprung most major urban parks in the United States." Paul Goldberger, the architecture critic of The New York Times, has ranked Central Park among the top ten architectural achievements in the city's history.

Possibly the Number One architectural achievement in the history of the world is the Manhattan skyline. It is a dream landscape that undulates from the towers of the financial district to the inspiring midtown mix of skyscrapers and on to the uptown apartment spires.

The first skyscrapers were built in Chicago on essentially swampy land but when the art came to New York, builders chose to anchor their towers to the solid rock that exists close to the surface from the tip of the Battery to about Canal Street and then emerges again at about 34th Street. The area in the middle, especially around Greenwich Village, is essentially marshy and criss-crossed by underground streams. The early tower builders avoided the problems of such terrain with the result that the major commercial centers leapfrogged some neighborhoods.

The same problem was considered when the first subway was built in 1904. The route ran from City Hall to the Upper West Side near Columbia University. The shortest line would have been straight up Broadway, but the engineers chose to run their line along the present route of the Lexington Avenue IRT. When they got to 42nd Street, they turned abruptly west, where the Times Square-Grand Central Shuttle runs today, and then continued on north when they hit Broadway.

The earliest skyscrapers were built near the southern end of that first subway line in the City Hall neighborhood, and the queen of them all, the Woolworth Building at 233 Broadway, just across the street from the Mayor's office, was the tallest building in the world from the day it opened in 1913 until the Chrysler Building was finished in 1930. At that time another tower at 40 Wall Street was also under construction and its promoters were telling the world that they were about to capture the title of tallest building in the world. The Chrysler people out-foxed them by adding a long slender spire to its graceful rounded top which made it 1047 feet high and gave it the tallest title until the 1472-foot Empire State Building was finished in 1931.

The Empire State held the world's record for tallness until the 1970s, when the twin towers of the World Trade Center pushed it down not once, but twice. The Trade Center towers were dedicated on April 5, 1973 but less than one month later they became the second (and third) tallest buildings in the world when a Chicago upstart called the Sears Tower topped out at 104 feet higher.

Back in the late 1940s, the architect and city planner Le Corbusier said that the New York skyline was "a catastrophe," but even from the point of view of his severe taste he had to admit it "a beautiful and worthy catastrophe." Noting that at that time the city as a vertical organism was not much more than 20 years old, he was enthusiastic about the idea that "New York has such courage and enthusiasm that everything can be begun again, sent back to the building yard and made into something still greater, something mastered!"

In 1963 many New Yorkers began hanging their heads in shame over their penchant for destroying the old to make way for the new, after the building that had housed Pennsylvania Station since 1910 was torn down to make way for a much less elegant, or useful, railroad station; an office tower that ignored its street address by calling itself "Penn Plaza" and a building resembling a bass drum turned over on its side that is home to The Madison Square Garden Center. It became the fourth site of The Garden, the first having been a converted car barn, that had served the Hudson and Harlem Railroad over on Madison Square at 26th Street and Madison

Avenue. The version of Madison Square Garden the latest one replaced, at Eighth Avenue and 50th Street, is still nothing more than a parking lot after 20 years.

When Penn Station disappeared, New Yorkers began asking themselves if it was such a smart idea to send the City's fine old buildings "back to the building yard." The result was a strong Landmarks Preservation law that helps protect the exteriors of important buildings and even some entire neighborhoods. The effort, and some of its results, gave a boost to other cities who saw the wisdom of "recycling" old buildings rather than tearing them down.

It also produced a wave of nostalgia and a longing for "the good old days." But how good were they?

Back in the 1880s after they arrested a small-timer named Piker Ryan, police found a price list in his pocket that ranged from a $2 fee for a simple punching to double that much for blackening both eyes, to $25 to stab someone. He really was a piker. A few years later the city's huge underworld came under control of a character named Monk Eastman, whose neck and face carried a dozen or more scars from knife wounds. He liked to tell people that he had been shot so often that he had to make allowances for the bullets in his body when he weighed himself. Ambulance drivers called the emergency room at Bellevue Hospital "The Eastman Pavilion." By the turn of the century he was the undisputed king of the underworld, controlling literally hundreds of people on the streets picking pockets, snatching handbags and generally keeping the citizenry on edge while keeping rival gangs at bay. It was the high point of gang control of the city, a virtual reign of terror that had begun just before the Civil War and didn't end until the early 1930s, when the LaGuardia landslide in the Mayoral election put Tammany Hall out of business once and for all and removed the likes of Monk Eastman from behind their political protection.

But if the city wasn't nearly as safe in "the good old days," was it more fun?

There is no denying they knew how to have a good time in the years between the Civil War and World War I. In the 1860s Mark Twain grumbled that "the city has grown too large." In 1868 a French journalist reported ". . . About 20 theaters, including minstrel halls, are open to the public every night and the opera and the drama are there interpreted in divers pleasing ways to suit all tastes. As regards drinking saloons, their number is beyond calculation."

During the same period an English journalist ventured out to Coney Island and reported: "They spread out over the four miles of sand strip with bands of music in full blast. Countless vehicles are moving; all the miniature theaters, minstrel shows, merry-go-rounds, Punch and Judy enterprises, fat women, big snakes, giant, dwarf and midget exhibitions, circuses and menageries, swings, flying horses and fortune-telling shops are open; and everywhere a dense but good-humored crowd, sightseeing, drinking beer and swallowing clam chowder."

It was the era of Diamond Jim Brady and "The" Mrs. Astor, of opulent banquets in restaurants like Delmonicos and Sherry's and feasts in Broadway lobster palaces like Rector's and Shanley's.

Looking back on it, it does seem like fun and, as always, the most fun was right here in New York City.

But it was also the time when newspaperman Jacob Riis took a hard look at the immigrant neighborhoods on the Lower East Side and found that there were 330,000 people per square mile "content to live in pig sties submitting to robbery at the hands of the rent collector without a murmer."

But in spite of what the nostalgists say, New York is probably a better place right now than it has been at any time in its history. The streets are safer, and, yes, even less congested than they were 100 years ago. The food is better and more varied. And so is the entertainment. The best part is that it is still changing. It is still, Landmark Law or no, the only city in the world that tears itself down every ten years and builds a new city. It is the only place on earth where a native can go off on a two-week vacation and find his neighborhood changed when he gets back. It is the only place on earth that can say it is all things to all people and mean it.

After he moved to New York in the 1960s, the Irish poet, playwright and institution, Brendan Behan said: "We don't come to a city to be alone, and the test of a city is the ease with which you can see and talk to the people. A city is a place where you are least likely to get a bite from a wild sheep and I'd say New York is the friendliest city I know."

Almost anyone who's never been to New York thrives on myths like the one that says New Yorkers aren't friendly.

"People live in those big apartment houses for years," they tell you, "and never get to know their next-door neighbor. You could die there and nobody would care." The fact is that most New Yorkers do know their neighbors and many of them know as much about their neighbors as anybody in any small town where all the neighbors are often related to each other. The difference is that when space is limited, people have a tendency to respect each other's space. New Yorkers are very good at that, but they do care about each other.

The city is broken down into convenient neighborhoods and anybody who has lived in one for more than a few weeks is probably on a first-name basis with the dry-cleaner, the newsstand operator, the supermarket checkout clerk. They have genuine sympathy for the shoe repair man whose landlord has just raised his rent to $2500 a month. They have their favorite neighborhood restaurants where they know they'll meet good friends on evenings when cooking doesn't seem like the perfect ending to a busy day. When they're out jogging or walking the dog it's inevitable that they'll stop for a minute or two to have a chat with a neighbor about what's going to happen to that expensive storefront now that the shoemaker has moved out and the conversation will probably lead to information about where to get their running shoes repaired now that he's gone.

Out-of-towners get a taste of New York friendliness, and pride, simply by standing on a midtown corner with a confused look. Even native New Yorkers who seem not to know where they're going will find themselves surrounded by people eager to help them. Anyone who stands on a New York street studying a guide book or a map is certain to be approached with an offer of help. Sometimes the advice is wrong, of course; even the natives don't always know that the Number Four bus on Madison Avenue will eventually get you all the way uptown to the Cloisters or that the best way to get from Grand Central Terminal to Penn Station is to walk over to Fifth Avenue and take the same Number Four bus to the other end of the line.

Though public transportation can get you anywhere you want to go in New York City, the best way to see it and capture its spirit is on foot. There are those who live in New York who still don't know that, but during a recent transit strike thousands found out and since then the best way to spot a real New Yorker is to look for someone smartly dressed but wearing sneakers. Young women executives with trim skirts and blazers and with glasses casually perched on top of their heads usually have an extra tote bag added to the soft briefcase they always carry to accommodate their high-heeled shoes. The male executives always wear three-piece suits, of course, an interesting contrast to their sneakers.

What makes walking an adventure is the unbelievable variety of people and street scenes. On the Upper East Side, the folks who run the string of boutiques along Madison Avenue thoughtfully change their window displays once a week on the average. If your route takes you through the Garment Center, on Seventh Avenue below 42nd Street, you'll find many of the 300,000 people who work in the neighborhood at work on the street pushing bolts of cloth on hand trucks or finished dresses on wheeled racks from one building to another. You'll see the salesmen moving their samples in waist-high wheeled suitcases, and you'll pass knots of people stopped in the middle of the sidewalk trying to find out from each other "how's business?"

On the West Side, the people will be casually-dressed in studied costumes they hope make them look "creative." On the East Side your fellow-walkers will be more stylishly-dressed in outfits they know make them look "successful." Down in the Financial District everybody looks successful. In Greenwich Village and SoHo everybody looks young.

But wherever you go in New York, the people are interesting, if not beautiful. There's a vitality in the city that's infectuous. Even if they're not "making it," most New Yorkers are pleased to tell you that they expect they will be some day soon. And they're equally proud to tell you that making it in New York is a tough proposition. They're probably right, but at this moment there are more than seven million people taking the challenge and most of them wouldn't trade places with anyone.

New York may well be the only city in the world with a choice of 25,000 restaurants, where it's possible to have breakfast at a fine Danish restaurant, lunch at a Japanese sushi bar and dinner in an old-fashioned American place.

It's a shopper's paradise where anything that can be bought anywhere in the world is available, often at a discount. And the best part is that Manhattan itself is divided into districts that make it easier to find what you're looking for than is often possible in the arrangement of many fine department stores. Diamonds are on 47th Street, west of Fifth Avenue, or on the Bowery near Canal Street. You'll find discount hardware and hi-fi equipment down on Canal Street west of Broadway, musical instruments on Broadway above 60th Street across from Lincoln Center, Indian spices and even saris on Lexington Avenue above 23rd Street and exotic food you never dreamed existed down in Chinatown. Flowers are best bought on Sixth Avenue below 32nd Street, the best buys in cameras are in the same general area, and for fresh produce and good meat, the best place to go is Ninth Avenue above 35th Street.

But for shoppers the most fun of all is a Sunday afternoon on the Lower East Side around Orchard Street where thousands go every week to save big money on women's clothes, shoes and handbags. And the best part of that adventure is that you can go another block or two east and sample the food at a kosher Chinese restaurant or, better still, stop at an open-air shop and grab a big sour pickle right from a big oak barrel. One bite and you're in another world.

New York is another world. No other city anywhere quite compares with it. And it's getting better every day. It's a place people dream about, a place they bring their dreams to have them come true.

In fact, that's why they call New York City "The Big Apple." It all began with a dream:

Back in the days when big bands were the musical rage, they spread their fame by cruising around the country doing what they called "one-night stands." As soon as they finished playing in a place like Scranton, Pa., they'd board a bus and ride the width of Pennsylvania for their next date in Erie. The bus became their bedroom. Most tours lasted for weeks at a time and most musicians longed to sleep in a real bed.

The one place they knew that could happen was New York, where bands were playing in hotels, in theaters, in nightclubs. There were lots of big opportunities and the more they talked among themselves about it as the buses raced through the night, the more tempting it became to quit that job and take a chance with the big city. The temptation was no less irresistible than the one Eve faced back in the beginning and it wasn't long before the musicians, with their penchant for reducing everything to slang and code words, stopped talking about New York and began dreaming their dreams about "The Big Apple."

It's not just big. It's the Eighth Wonder of The World.

THE STATUE OF LIBERTY

Erected in 1886, the Statue, "Liberty Enlightening the World", was a gift from the people of France. United States citizens raised funds for the stone pedestal on which it stands. Conceived as a monument to the long friendship between France and the United States that began during the American Revolution, the Statue has become a beacon of hope for newcomers to America.

"A beacon of hope for newcomers to America," the Statue of Liberty, erected in 1886 as a first centenary gift from the French nation, stands at the entrance to New York City's harbor.

Seen from the Brooklyn docks, the dark shapes of the skyscrapers that comprise Manhattan's financial area stand out against the lowering evening sky *above*. Liberty Island, with its world famous statue *facing page*, is a popular tourist attraction.

The equestrian statue of General Sherman *center and far right* stands in Grand Army Plaza on Fifth Avenue, attracting artists *right* and rollerskaters *bottom right* to this pleasant location. Horse-drawn carriages *below* are a common sight in this part of the city, providing an almost therapeutic form of transport. Central Park's Sheep Meadow seen looking towards Manhattan's West Side *facing page* is a recreation area much loved by New Yorkers.

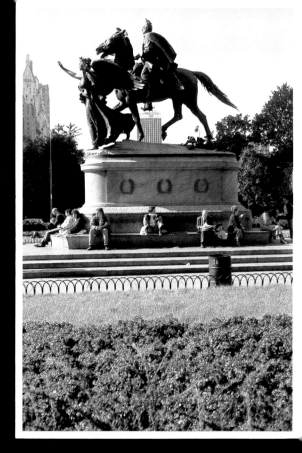

A spider's web of twisted cable and massive, twin-arched gothic pillars distinguish Brooklyn Bridge *right, bottom and facing page.* In all, three bridges as well as the Brooklyn Battery tunnel link the borough of Brooklyn to Manhattan, each handling an enormous volume of daily traffic. Silently perched on its island in Upper Bay of New York Harbor stands the Statue of Liberty *far right. Below:* a sea plane passes the Watchtower building, headquarters of the Jehovah's Witnesses organisation.

Previous pages left: **a calm East River reflects the golden glow of the office block lights and** *right* **the ubiquitous yellow cabs on Fifth Avenue.** *These pages:* **New York winters can be particularly severe and disruptive, bringing normal life to a virtual standstill and enveloping the city in an unnatural silence. Only necessity brings people out of doors onto the snow-laden streets, where skis become the ideal means of transport.**

The Guggenheim Museum *facing page,* **Frank Lloyd Wright's futuristic creation, stands on Fifth Avenue, at the center of what has come to be known as 'Museum Mile,' an area that boasts about 30 other such cultural institutions.** *This page:* **New York's glass and concrete mountains reflect and are reflected in every polished surface.**

Temporarily supreme, the twin towers of the World Trade Center dominate all other buildings on Lower Manhattan's skyline *above. Facing page:* looking north over a frozen Central Park.

Fifth Avenue *facing page*, New York's most elegant shopping area, is home to many internationally famous names *below*. Two of the city's many fine hotels: the Grand Hyatt *bottom right* and the Helmsley Palace *bottom left*. Left *and below left*: store fronts in Rockefeller Center. *Far left*: a wedding group on the steps of St Patrick's cathedral.

The Plaza *this page,* possibly the grandest of all New York hotels, stands at the intersection of 59th Street and Fifth Avenue. Although adjoining structures may now tower over it, the dignified Plaza retains its aura of greatness. *Facing page:* Central Park, seen from above, seems to hold back the advance of an army of skyscrapers.

Fine restaurants serving mouthwatering American and Continental dishes in luxurious surroundings help make New York a veritable gourmet's paradise. The magnificent Plaza Hotel *these pages* can itself offer a bewildering choice of dishes in settings as varied as the Oyster Bar, the Edwardian Room, the Oak Room and the Palm Court.

Guest's eye views of New York from the upper stories of the Plaza Hotel: the Pulitzer Fountain and the sunken plaza of the General Motors Building on Fifth Avenue *facing page.* Left: East 59th Street with the Queensboro Bridge in the distance and the statue of General Sherman and the imposing Pierre Hotel, with its French-style roof *below.*

Autumn's mellow colors add a warm richness to the vast expanse of Central Park, the tones of the vegetation echoed subtly in the shimmering waters of the lake. Apartment buildings that line the borders of the Park are amongst the most exclusive and expensive in the city, not least because of the pleasant views that they offer. The lake itself *these pages* is one of the Park's more popular amenities, serving both the recreational and contemplative needs of its visitors.

As the Park changes with the season, so too do the activities of the people, with winter sportsmen ready to take advantage of the first good fall of snow. Skiers, skaters, ice hockey players and the ubiquitous jogger are a common sight on the clear, crisp, sunny days. *Facing page:* looking west from Central Park, with the famous Dakota apartment building shown center of the picture at the park's West 72nd Street entrance.

In 1899 the conservationists finally lost their battle to prevent the incursion of automobile traffic into Central Park. Up until that time it had been the city's last bastion against the horseless carriage, the park commissioners having resolutely refused to issue permits to this new form of traffic. Despite and perhaps in part due to this inevitable progress, the sedate hansom cab continues to ferry visitors around the park's winding roads, where the fare buys a half-hour's worth of gentle relaxation. The original cabbies were traditionally expatriate London drivers, themselves having been forced out of work by the advent of the car. Some of the present day cabbies continue to wear the more sober traditional uniform of yesteryear.

Liberty Island and its statue *above* **was, to many travel weary immigrants, their first sight of the longed for promised land. Today, ferry boats bring tourists here to enjoy the views that the statue's lofty vantage points can offer.** *Facing page:* **Battery Park stands on the southern tip of Manhattan and it is from here that the ferry boats leave for the Statue of Liberty.**

Brooklyn Bridge *above,* 13 years in the making and finally completed in 1883 to John Roebling's design, is probably the best known of all the New York bridges. Looking west from the shores of Roosevelt Island on East River can be seen the United Nations Building *facing page left* and the spires of the Empire State Building center and Chrysler Building right.

Grand Central Station *these pages,* nestling beneath the awesome bulk of the Pan Am Building, is New York's prime railroad staging post. From here, trains leave for such destinations as Boston, Chicago, Albany, Connecticut and even Canada.

Facing page: **the Empire State and her sister skyscrapers appear spotlit by the dying embers of the sun, while in the foreground, a shaded Greenwich Village stretches to the arch in Washington Square.** *Above:* **light-speckled slabs of steel and concrete stand silhouetted against an orange evening sky.**

As in all cities, the demand for taxi cabs increases with the first signs of rain. *Far right:* Park Avenue looking north and *bottom right* an uncommonly deserted Sixth Avenue, also known as the Avenue of the Americas. *Facing page:* a busy Fifth Avenue looking south. *Overleaf:* characters and everyday life in the bustling city of New York.

A myriad pin pricks of light glow from the dark and varied shapes of the city buildings, endowing them with an uncharacteristic delicacy. The colored lights crowning the Empire State Building *far right and facing page* are changed with the seasons, shown here in the national colors of red white and blue for the Independence Day celebrations.

New York's Chinatown, although quite small compared to that of San Francisco, is an important and integral part of the city's varied character. Occupying a few blocks of south Manhattan, Chinatown's food shops, stalls and restaurants serve both the visitor and its own community.

To the outsider with a love for oriental cuisine, Chinatown has a special appeal, yet to the 6000 Americans of Chinese extraction who live here, this is home. The streets of the area ring to the unfamiliar sounds of Chinese voices and the air is filled with the mouthwatering aroma of oriental cooking. Shop fronts, tantalisingly stacked with gold colored duck, chicken, pork and octopus are a trap for the hungry passer-by, and well stocked fish shops boast an incredible variety of fresh sea food.

Manhattan's buildings *above,* seen from the New Jersey piers, appear to huddle together for warmth under the sullen gray winter sky, while a sleek sailing boat *facing page,* moored on the Brooklyn side of East River, provides a contrast with the modern backdrop.

Facing page: an aerial view of downtown New York, with the famous Flatiron building standing at the intersection of **23rd Street, Broadway and Fifth Avenue.** *Above:* **Flanked by Fifth Avenue to the right, with Washington Square at its southern end, and Sixth Avenue to the left, is the proud Empire State Building. The lights of the George Washington Bridge can be seen in the top left corner of the picture.**

Central Park, resplendent in Autumn's rich colors *these pages*, stands in 840 acres of central Manhattan. Walled in on all four sides by the city's skyscrapers, this rectangular piece of land has, since its completion in 1876, played an important part in the lives of all New Yorkers. The park's varied and ever increasing attractions now include sports, recreational and cultural facilities that cater for most tastes.

I BELIEVE IN THE SUPREME WORTH OF THE INDIVIDUAL
AND IN HIS RIGHT TO LIFE, LIBERTY AND THE PURSUIT OF HAPPINESS

I BELIEVE
THAT EVERY RIGHT IMPLIES A RESPONSIBILITY; EVERY
OPPORTUNITY, AN OBLIGATION; EVERY POSSESSION, A DUTY

I BELIEVE
THAT THE LAW WAS MADE FOR MAN AND NOT MAN FOR THE
LAW; THAT GOVERNMENT IS THE SERVANT OF THE PEOPLE
AND NOT THEIR MASTER

I BELIEVE
IN THE DIGNITY OF LABOR, WHETHER WITH HEAD OR HAND;
THAT THE WORLD OWES NO MAN A LIVING BUT THAT IT
OWES EVERY MAN AN OPPORTUNITY TO MAKE A LIVING

I BELIEVE
THAT THRIFT IS ESSENTIAL TO WELL ORDERED LIVING
AND THAT ECONOMY IS A PRIME REQUISITE OF A SOUND
FINANCIAL STRUCTURE, WHETHER IN GOVERNMENT,
BUSINESS OR PERSONAL AFFAIRS

I BELIEVE
THAT TRUTH AND JUSTICE ARE FUNDAMENTAL TO AN
ENDURING SOCIAL ORDER

I BELIEVE
IN THE SACREDNESS OF A PROMISE, THAT A MAN'S WORD
SHOULD BE AS GOOD AS HIS BOND; THAT CHARACTER-NOT
WEALTH OR POWER OR POSITION-IS OF SUPREME WORTH

I BELIEVE
THAT THE RENDERING OF USEFUL SERVICE IS THE COMMON
DUTY OF MANKIND AND THAT ONLY IN THE PURIFYING FIRE
OF SACRIFICE IS THE DROSS OF SELFISHNESS CONSUMED
AND THE GREATNESS OF THE HUMAN SOUL SET FREE

I BELIEVE
IN AN ALL-WISE AND ALL-LOVING GOD, NAMED BY
WHATEVER NAME, AND THAT THE INDIVIDUAL'S HIGHEST
FULFILLMENT, GREATEST HAPPINESS, AND WIDEST
USEFULNESS ARE TO BE FOUND IN LIVING IN HARMONY
WITH HIS WILL

I BELIEVE
THAT LOVE IS THE GREATEST THING IN THE WORLD;
THAT IT ALONE CAN OVERCOME HATE; THAT
CAN AND WILL TRIUMPH OVER MIGHT

JOHN·D·ROCKEFELLER·JR

John D. Rockefeller's personal philosophy, immortalized in marble *above,* **is fittingly one of the Rockefeller Center's major attractions, together with the splendid Paul Manship statue of Prometheus** *facing page,* **which stands at the opposite end of the center's skating rink.**

A majestic, light-bejeweled
Christmas tree in the Channel
Gardens complements the
Rockefeller Center's superb festive
decorations and is rivaled only by
the sparkling trees near the Tavern
on the Green in Central Park *above*.

The World Trade Center's upper stories offer superb views *facing page* **of the city's midtown area, while from the top of the Empire State Building the scenes** *above* **appear somewhat more intimate.**

The best way of seeing and appreciating New York's many varied sights is to do what the natives do and walk. For the foot-weary traveler with limited time, however, buses, cabs, limousines and even bicycles are the logical alternative.

Flags, yellow cabs as well as fruit and vegetable stalls add a touch of color to the street scenes between Times Square and Wall Street *this page*. The seat of New York power, three-tiered City Hall *facing page* is topped by a figure bearing the scales of justice.

The corner of 42nd Street and Eighth Avenue *these pages* is one of the city's busiest if less attractive intersections. For the visitor interested in sampling the sights of the area, Times Square, just one block further east, has much more to offer.

New York has more fine vantage points than any other city in the world and the RCA Building's Rainbow Room
nightclub is one of these. From here the uptown view *above* is stunning and the downtown aspect *facing page* equally
impressive

Well over a million Americans with Italian backgrounds live in New York, and Little Italy, with its popular restaurants proudly proclaiming their heritage *above*, is where many of their forefathers first settled. Nearby Washington Square *top right* and its small park provides an open space for relaxation and assignations. The flavor of Chinatown *right and far right*, although a contrast, is no less pleasing. Much has been said regarding the risks of traveling on New York's subways *facing page*, yet despite this they are an efficient and much used form of transport.

Castle Clinton National Monument

Battery Park

Fire Dept. Pier

Battery Park City

Signs on the windows *facing page* at the top of the **World Trade Center** *far right* help the uninformed in identifying the sights below. There is little that cannot be seen from this quarter-mile high observatory, where telescopes are provided *top right* for the convenience of the visitor. The mirrored corridor *top* and the round windows *above* of the **Empire State Building** give a better view of the midtown area.

From street level, the Gothic spires of St. Patrick's Cathedral *left* appear immensely tall and yet, seen from the heights of the Rockefeller Center's RCA Building the cruciform structure seems strangely small *far left. Below:* a reverent silence pervades the Main Reading Room of the Public Library, where bowed figures devote themselves to study. In summer months the sunken Plaza of the Rockefeller Center is transformed from skating rink to open air cafe *facing page.*

On Thanksgiving Day, inflated comic characters such as Snoopy *facing page* and Kermit the Frog *bottom center* take to the streets as part of the Macy's parade. Parades and festivals, such as the Hispanic one held on Columbus Day, apart from being happy and colorful occasions, are ideal opportunities for the ethnic minorities to take a pride in themselves and their richly varied backgrounds.

The majestic Citicorp Center occupies a block bounded by Lexington and Third Avenues and 53rd and 54th Streets. With the elegant seven storey Atrium at its center *bottom right*, the complex boasts many fine shops and amenities as well as the pleasant plaza outside *below*. Equally imposing are the Ford Foundation's enclosed gardens *right*, *far right* *and bottom center* on 42nd Street and the McGraw-Hill Plaza in Rockefeller Center *facing page*.

THE LORD JESUS CHRIST DIED TO SAVE SINNERS - HE DIED TO SAVE YOU!

FRANKFURTERS & ROLLS

SABRETT

Hot dog, drink and pretzel stands serve almost as first aid points for the hungry crowds that pack the Lower East Side each Sunday in search of a bargain. For those who need it, even salvation is on offer *top.*

As much a work of art as the objects that it houses, the Guggenheim Museum *right and facing page,* with its gently winding floors, contains a fine collection of contemporary art. The Museum of Modern Art *above, top left and center* is packed with the works of countless famous artists while the staid Metropolitan Museum *top right,* ranks as one of the finest repositories of treasure in the world.

Five boroughs combined make up the city of New York, and yet it is the smallest of these – Manhattan – that sums up the essence of the city to the outsider. However you look at it; from under the Brooklyn Bridge *top left*; from Liberty Island *left*; from a Brooklyn pier *above*; from a boat off Battery Park *top* or from the top of a skyscraper *facing page*, there can be no denying that this man-made landscape is breathtaking.

Not a square at all, in the true sense of the word, Times Square *these pages,* at the intersection of Broadway, 42nd Street and Seventh Avenue, is the pulsating if somewhat gaudy heart of the entertainment district. Posters, giant signs and flashing lights proclaim the attractions of the non-stop excitement which democratically caters for every imaginable taste.

These pages: **whether you are a visitor or a native to New York, the chances are that if Fifth Avenue's traffic doesn't stop you, its sights and sounds will.**

Sixty-five bridges serve the island of Manhattan, radiating from its banks towards the neighboring boroughs like the spokes of some enormous wheel. The Queensboro Bridge *right*, which runs into 59th Street, was completed in 1909 and the Manhattan Bridge *facing page* was opened in the same year.
If big is indeed beautiful, then there can be no disputing that the identical twins that comprise the World Trade Center *far right and below* are just that. From the observation deck on the 107th floor those with a head for heights can enjoy unbeatable views. *Bottom right:* the sleek Citicorp Building.

New York lays claim to some 25,000 restaurants of varying standards. These can range from the inexpensive but welcoming neighborhood bar *facing page* where you can enjoy a drink and snack with a friend, to the more exclusive places such as the Crystal Room at the Tavern on the Green *bottom center* or the Sign of the Dove *left. Bottom right*: the Metropolitan Opera House at Lincoln Center.

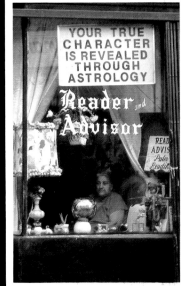

The intimate, small-town atmosphere of Greenwich Village *these pages* lives on thanks to the preservation of its older buildings. The streets are full of surprises and well worth exploring. *Facing page:* this row of houses in Grove Court stand back to back with a similar row on Grove Street.

The Rockefeller Center *these pages*, a daring pre-war undertaking that seems to luxuriate in its open space, is composed of a number of lesser buildings gathered around the central 70-storey RCA Building *far right*, beneath which stands the famous statue of Prometheus *bottom right*. A feature of the Center is its sunken plaza, which serves as a restaurant in the summer *bottom center* and an ice rink in the winter *facing page*. The Channel Gardens *below* form an impressive entrance to the Center from Fifth Avenue where the statue of Atlas *right* can be seen at the base of the International Building.

Whatever your needs, be it a haircut *facing page*, a shoeshine *right*, a quick repair job *far right and below*, newspaper *center right* or bagel *bottom right*, the chances are that you will soon find some enterprising character eager to serve you. The city is packed with modest one-man businesses whose prices are likely to prove pleasantly surprising; you may even get some useful information into the bargain!

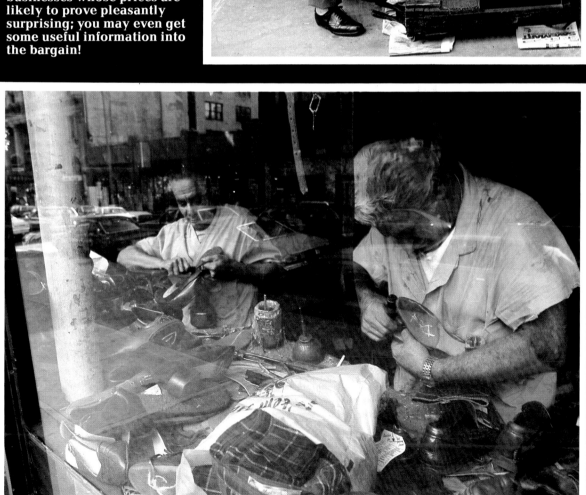

Cheap jewelry *left* and croissants *top left* are not the only things you will find for sale on the streets. On Saturday nights, while you are walking the dogs *above*, you can always buy a copy of the next morning's Sunday Times on many a Manhattan corner. *Facing page:* a typical New York ticker tape parade.

123

The Citicorp Building's elegant Atrium, surrounded by equally impressive, well stocked stores, is the ideal place to meet friends or relax during a shopping trip. If the smell of fresh-baked bread from the Au Pain Bakery *left* makes you feel hungry then you can always enjoy a nutritional meal at Healthworks *far left*.

The endless variety of the facades is one of the characteristics of New York. *Top, left to right:* the Pan Am Building, the Municipal Building and the Crossroads Building at Times Square. *Above, left to right:* an Upper West Side apartment house, the Flatiron Building and the Standard Oil Building. Shown *facing page* is the glass front of the Grand Hyatt Hotel.

The Urban Park Rangers *these pages* who patrol Central Park on horseback, are a constant reminder of the area's more sinister side. In former days it was not uncommon for people to spend a summer night here under the stars. Today, only the foolhardy venture there unaccompanied after dark. As well as keeping the peace, the Rangers also serve as guides, offering useful assistance to the visitors.

Even Manhattan's man made wonders cannot rival the natural beauty of a sunset over Upper New York Bay *above.*
Facing page: **Liberty Island, flanked by Governor's Island to the left and Ellis Island to the right, with the Verrazano-Narrows Bridge linking Brooklyn to Staten Island in the distance.**

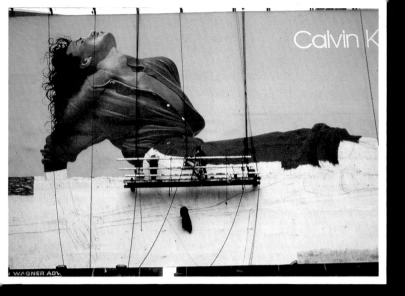

Facing page: **one could be forgiven for thinking that all cars in New York are this color. Huge advertisements** *top left and top center* **and neon signs** *far left* **compete for space with the imaginative neighborhood murals** *top.* **The conservative frontages of the Italian Bakery** *far left center* **and Mamma Leone's Restaurant** *above* **contrast strongly with the brashness of the fast food outlet** *left.*

The Mall *facing page* is one of Central Park's broadest avenues. It leads to the beautiful Bethesda Fountain and boating lake *left.* Considerably smaller, but no less charming is Bryant Park shown *below* with its formal balustrades.

Each Sunday, hordes of bargain hunters flock into Orchard Street on the Lower East Side *these pages*, where shops and stalls overflowing with cheap clothes do a brisk trade. Even if you don't wish to buy, the visit can be quite an experience.

Mounted police *top left and facing page* preserve the peace and control the crowds that converge nightly onto Broadway and Times Square *left and above* in search of entertainment. *Top:* a flea market held in a vacant lot.

The area south of Houston Street, commonly refered to as SoHo, has in recent times like Greenwich Village, become one of the fashionable centers of Bohemian life where galleries, exhibiting somewhat unconventional works of art *this page,* abound. *Facing page:* looking for all the world like a conventional New York factory building, this prefabricated cast-iron frontage owes more to the spanner-wielding workman than the bricklayer. Relatively quick and cheap to erect, cast-iron buildings went through a boom period during the mid-1850s but the trend did not endure.

ROSARIO RAVA
& SONS, INC.

TEXTILE WASTES

28-30

Exuding solid respectability, the neo-classical facade of the New York Stock Exchange *below* belies the technology within, where a mass of monitors display the latest market information to the teeming crowd of traders *bottom left and facing page. Left:* Downtown Manhattan and the Brooklyn Bridge.

Like moths to a flame, entertainment seekers flock to the bright lights of Times Square *left, top left and facing page. Above:* Lexington Avenue and the characteristic shape of the Chrysler Building.

147

Skyscrapers in the truest sense, Manhattan's tallest structures *above* **pierce a layer of cloud. Yamasaki's twin towers**
facing page, **whilst not the most elegant of buildings, certainly reflect the self confidence of the city that plays host to them.**

Walter Scott *facing page,* clutching a thoughtfully provided bouquet, sits at the end of Central Park's Mall watching the enthusiastic joggers *above, top right and far right* as well as the Park Rangers *top center* perform their daily tasks. *Right:* a Fifth Avenue sidewalk, where cyclists and pedestrians compete for space.

The Alice in Wonderland figures *top left and top right*, which stand near the Central Park Model Boat Basin *above*, are always popular with children. For the adults the fresh air and a moment's peace are often enough.

ITALIAN SAUSAGES
PEPPERS & ONIONS

SHISH-KEBAB 1.25
SOUVLAKI ON PITA 1.75
WITH LETTUCE & TOMATO
ALL BEEF FRANKS 65¢
HOT SAUSAGE 85¢
HOT KNISH 60¢
ICE COLD SODA 60¢
HOT PRETZEL 50¢
N.Y. TRAILER

HOT FRESH PRETZELS 60¢

Cafés and restaurants, as well as the more modest food vendor's stands, assault the senses of the passer-by with their sights and smells. It can take a considerable degree of self-control to pass by without at least being tempted – the chances are that you will succumb.

National emblems on the street lamps are a feature of the Avenue of the Americas – Sixth Avenue *facing page* – Greenwich Village's prime thoroughfare. *Below:* reflections in one of the many unusual and interesting shop windows to be found in the Village. *Left, far left and bottom left:* fire escapes form a zig-zag pattern on the fronts of brightly colored tenement buildings.

A crowded boat *above* ferries sightseers to Liberty Island. On a clear night, the symbolic flame of the statue's torch *facing page* can be seen from a considerable distance. *Overleaf:* the wooden walkway of the Brooklyn Bridge.